A Traveler's Weekly Planner

Lay the Foundation

for Your Weeks Experiences

Activinotes

Activinotes

DAILY JOURNALS, PLANNERS, NOTEBOOKS AND OTHER BLANK BOOKS

Copyright 2016

Weekly **Planner**

Travel

MONDAY	TUESDAY	WEDNESDAY	To Do List

THURSDAY	FRIDAY	SATURDAY	To Buy List

SUNDAY			To Do List

Weekly  Planner

_____

_____

_____

_____

Weekly  Planner

Weekly Planner

Travel

MONDAY	TUESDAY	WEDNESDAY	To Do List

THURSDAY	FRIDAY	SATURDAY	To Buy List

SUNDAY			To Do List

Weekly *Travel* Planner

_____
_____
_____
_____

Weekly  Planner

Weekly  *Planner*

MONDAY	TUESDAY	WEDNESDAY	To Do List

THURSDAY	FRIDAY	SATURDAY	To Buy List

SUNDAY			To Do List

Weekly  Planner

_____

_____

_____

_____

Weekly  Planner

Weekly Planner

Travel

MONDAY	TUESDAY	WEDNESDAY	To Do List

THURSDAY	FRIDAY	SATURDAY	To Buy List

SUNDAY	To Do List

Weekly Planner

Travel

Weekly  Planner

Weekly  Planner

MONDAY	TUESDAY	WEDNESDAY	To Do List

THURSDAY	FRIDAY	SATURDAY	To Buy List

SUNDAY	To Do List

Weekly  Planner

_____
_____
_____
_____

Weekly  Planner

Weekly Planner

Travel

MONDAY	TUESDAY	WEDNESDAY	To Do List

THURSDAY	FRIDAY	SATURDAY	To Buy List

SUNDAY	To Do List

Weekly  Planner

Weekly Planner

Travel

Travel

Weekly  Planner

Travel

MONDAY	TUESDAY	WEDNESDAY	To Do List

THURSDAY	FRIDAY	SATURDAY	To Buy List

SUNDAY			To Do List

Weekly Planner

Weekly  Planner

Weekly  Planner

MONDAY	TUESDAY	WEDNESDAY	To Do List

THURSDAY	FRIDAY	SATURDAY	To Buy List

SUNDAY		To Do List

Weekly i Travel *Planner*

_____
_____
_____
_____

Weekly  Planner

Weekly  *Planner*

MONDAY	TUESDAY	WEDNESDAY	To Do List

THURSDAY	FRIDAY	SATURDAY	To Buy List

SUNDAY		To Do List

Weekly  Planner

_____
_____
_____
_____

Weekly  Planner

Weekly  Planner

MONDAY	TUESDAY	WEDNESDAY	To Do List

THURSDAY	FRIDAY	SATURDAY	To Buy List

SUNDAY			To Do List

Weekly  Planner

_____
_____
_____
_____

Weekly  Planner

Weekly Travel Planner

MONDAY	TUESDAY	WEDNESDAY	To Do List

THURSDAY	FRIDAY	SATURDAY	To Buy List

SUNDAY	To Do List

Weekly  Planner

Weekly Planner

Travel

Travel

Weekly  Planner

MONDAY	TUESDAY	WEDNESDAY	To Do List

THURSDAY	FRIDAY	SATURDAY	To Buy List

SUNDAY		To Do List

Weekly Planner

Travel

Weekly  Planner

Weekly  Planner

MONDAY	TUESDAY	WEDNESDAY	To Do List

THURSDAY	FRIDAY	SATURDAY	To Buy List

SUNDAY		To Do List

Weekly  Planner

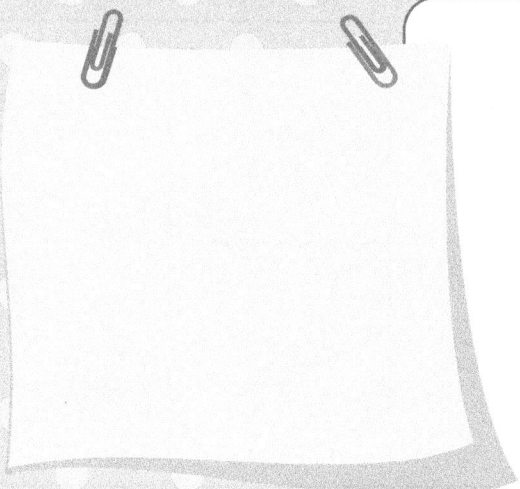

Weekly  Planner

Weekly Planner

Travel

MONDAY	TUESDAY	WEDNESDAY	To Do List

THURSDAY	FRIDAY	SATURDAY	To Buy List

SUNDAY	To Do List

Weekly Planner

i Travel

Weekly  Planner

Weekly  Planner

MONDAY	TUESDAY	WEDNESDAY	To Do List

THURSDAY	FRIDAY	SATURDAY	To Buy List

SUNDAY			To Do List

Weekly  Planner

_____
_____
_____
_____

Weekly Planner

Travel

Travel

Weekly *Travel* Planner

MONDAY	TUESDAY	WEDNESDAY	To Do List

THURSDAY	FRIDAY	SATURDAY	To Buy List

SUNDAY	To Do List

Weekly Planner

Travel

Weekly Planner

Travel

Weekly  *Planner*

MONDAY	TUESDAY	WEDNESDAY	To Do List

THURSDAY	FRIDAY	SATURDAY	To Buy List

SUNDAY		To Do List

Weekly  Planner

Weekly  Planner

Weekly Planner

Travel

MONDAY	TUESDAY	WEDNESDAY	To Do List

THURSDAY	FRIDAY	SATURDAY	To Buy List

SUNDAY		To Do List

Weekly  Planner

Weekly Planner

Travel

Weekly Travel Planner

MONDAY	TUESDAY	WEDNESDAY	To Do List

THURSDAY	FRIDAY	SATURDAY	To Buy List

SUNDAY	To Do List

Weekly  Planner

_____
_____
_____
_____

Weekly Planner

Travel

Travel

Weekly  Planner

MONDAY	TUESDAY	WEDNESDAY	To Do List

THURSDAY	FRIDAY	SATURDAY	To Buy List

SUNDAY	To Do List

Weekly

i Travel

Planner

Weekly  Planner

Weekly  Planner

MONDAY	TUESDAY	WEDNESDAY	To Do List

THURSDAY	FRIDAY	SATURDAY	To Buy List

SUNDAY	To Do List

Weekly  Planner

Weekly  Planner

Weekly Planner

Travel

MONDAY	TUESDAY	WEDNESDAY	To Do List

THURSDAY	FRIDAY	SATURDAY	To Buy List

SUNDAY	To Do List

Weekly Planner

_____

_____

_____

_____

Weekly  Planner

Weekly  Planner

MONDAY	TUESDAY	WEDNESDAY	To Do List

THURSDAY	FRIDAY	SATURDAY	To Buy List

SUNDAY		To Do List

Weekly  Planner

_____

_____

_____

_____

Weekly  Planner

Weekly  Planner

MONDAY	TUESDAY	WEDNESDAY	To Do List

THURSDAY	FRIDAY	SATURDAY	To Buy List

SUNDAY		To Do List

Weekly

i Travel

Planner

Weekly  Planner

Weekly Planner

Travel

MONDAY	TUESDAY	WEDNESDAY	To Do List

THURSDAY	FRIDAY	SATURDAY	To Buy List

SUNDAY			To Do List

Weekly  Planner

Travel

Weekly  Planner

Weekly Planner

Travel

MONDAY	TUESDAY	WEDNESDAY	To Do List

THURSDAY	FRIDAY	SATURDAY	To Buy List

SUNDAY	To Do List

Weekly Planner

Travel

_____
_____
_____
_____

Weekly  Planner

Weekly  Travel Planner

MONDAY	TUESDAY	WEDNESDAY	To Do List

THURSDAY	FRIDAY	SATURDAY	To Buy List

SUNDAY		To Do List

Weekly  Planner

Travel

Weekly Travel Planner

Travel

Weekly  *Planner*

Travel

MONDAY	TUESDAY	WEDNESDAY	To Do List

THURSDAY	FRIDAY	SATURDAY	To Buy List

SUNDAY			To Do List

Weekly Planner

Travel

Weekly  Planner

Weekly  Planner

MONDAY	TUESDAY	WEDNESDAY	To Do List

THURSDAY	FRIDAY	SATURDAY	To Buy List

SUNDAY			To Do List

Weekly  Planner

Weekly  Planner

Weekly  Planner

MONDAY	TUESDAY	WEDNESDAY	To Do List

THURSDAY	FRIDAY	SATURDAY	To Buy List

SUNDAY			To Do List

Weekly Planner

Travel

Weekly  Planner

Weekly Planner

Travel

MONDAY	TUESDAY	WEDNESDAY	To Do List

THURSDAY	FRIDAY	SATURDAY	To Buy List

SUNDAY		To Do List

Weekly  Planner

Weekly Planner

Travel

Travel

Weekly  Planner

MONDAY	TUESDAY	WEDNESDAY	To Do List

THURSDAY	FRIDAY	SATURDAY	To Buy List

SUNDAY	To Do List

Weekly  Planner

_____

_____

_____

_____

Weekly  Planner

Weekly Travel Planner

MONDAY	TUESDAY	WEDNESDAY	To Do List

THURSDAY	FRIDAY	SATURDAY	To Buy List

SUNDAY	To Do List

Weekly  Planner

Weekly  Planner

Weekly Travel Planner

MONDAY	TUESDAY	WEDNESDAY	To Do List

THURSDAY	FRIDAY	SATURDAY	To Buy List

SUNDAY	To Do List

Weekly Planner

Travel

Weekly  Planner

Notes

www.ingramcontent.com/pod-product-compliance
Lightning Source LLC
Chambersburg PA
CBHW081333090426
42737CB00017B/3122